Ready, set, draw! SEA CREATURES

WILLIAM POTTER & JUAN CALLE

ARCTURUS

ARCTURUS

This edition published in 2018 by Arcturus Publishing Limited
26/27 Bickels Yard, 151–153 Bermondsey Street,
London SE1 3HA

ISBN: 978-1-78428-982-9
CH005805NT
Supplier 29, Date 0518, Print run 6200

Art by Juan Calle, Colour by Luis Suarez (Liberum Donum)
Text by William Potter
Edited by Joe Harris

Printed in China

CONTENTS

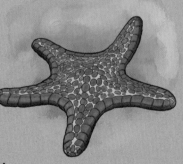

GETTING STARTED

THE STEPS

This book shows how you can draw a realistic sea creature starting with simple shapes. You can then add in detail, such as fins, tails, and scales.

The first step shows the basic building blocks for the body—circles, ovals, and curved lines—and the position of fins.

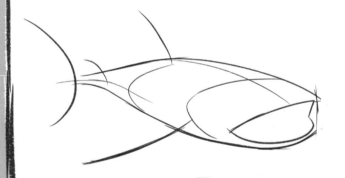

The second step refines these simple shapes and adds detail, such as the eyes and mouth. New lines are in blue as a guide. When you have drawn these outlines, you can erase the working lines you drew in step 1.

Later steps add extra detail, including gills, teeth, and skin patterns.

The final step is a guide to what shades you should use to complete your picture.

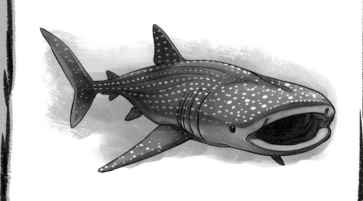

WHALES, SHARKS, AND DOLPHINS

SPERM WHALE

This giant of the deep sea has a rectangular head.

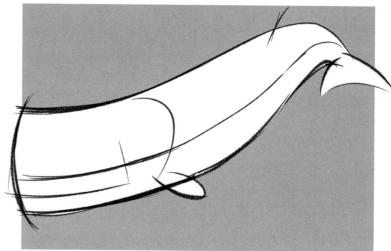

1. Draw a slightly curved sausage shape, with a wide flat end for the head and a point toward the back. Add a tail and fin.

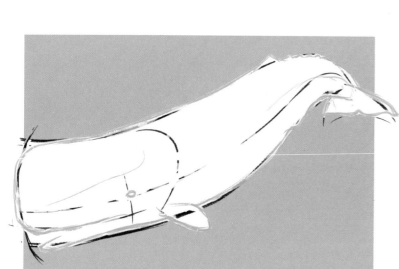

2. Add small bumps on the back, a triangle notch in the tail fin, and a tiny eye just behind and above the mouth.

3. Use short lines to mark wrinkles on the whale's skin, then add teeth in the open mouth.

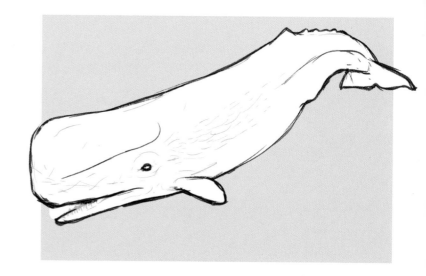

4. Paint your sperm whale in dark blue tones, then add a paler blue shine along its upper body and the top edge of the fins.

TOP TIP

The sperm whale has wrinkly skin. Use light tones, called highlights, where the sun lights the upper edges. Add shadows below to bring out the shape of these skin folds.

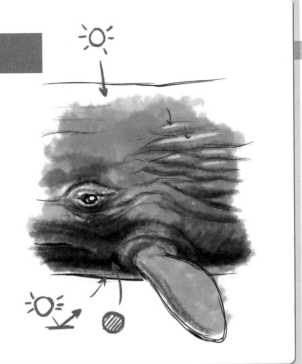

DOLPHIN

This acrobatic marine mammal is launching itself out of the water.

1. Sketch a slightly curved fish shape with a pointed nose and crescent tail fin. Mark the head, the nose, and where the other fins will go.

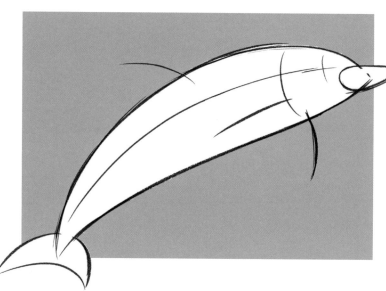

2. Shape the back and side fins. Position the eye, and draw a line for the dolphin's mouth.

3. Erase your working lines, then mark the edges of this common dolphin's dark patterns.

4. Paint the dark areas, then the pale areas with a tan shade. You could add a splash of water below the leaping dolphin.

TOP TIP

To draw splashing water, follow the movement of the dolphin, making the water's edges curve away from its body. Give the splash a rippled edge, adding a few extra drips.

HAMMERHEAD SHARK

This striking sea predator has an odd-looking flat head with eyes on either end.

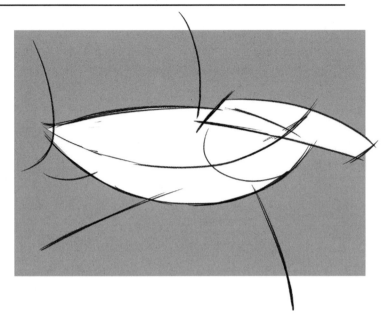

1. Outline an oval with pointed ends for the body. Indicate the fin positions. Add a curved rectangle for the head.

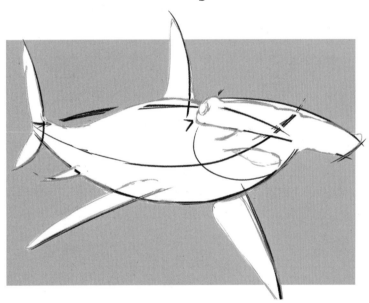

2. Shape the triangular fins. Add a rippled edge to the front of the head and an eye at one end. Draw an open mouth below the head.

3. Add the back fins and then the five gill slits behind the head. Draw the sharp teeth then add lines dividing the front of the head.

4. Paint this shark using a bright blue with a paler blue on its underside. Add highlights to the head and fins.

WILD FACT!
The bizarre shape of this shark's head is thought to help it locate weak electrical signals given off by its prey.

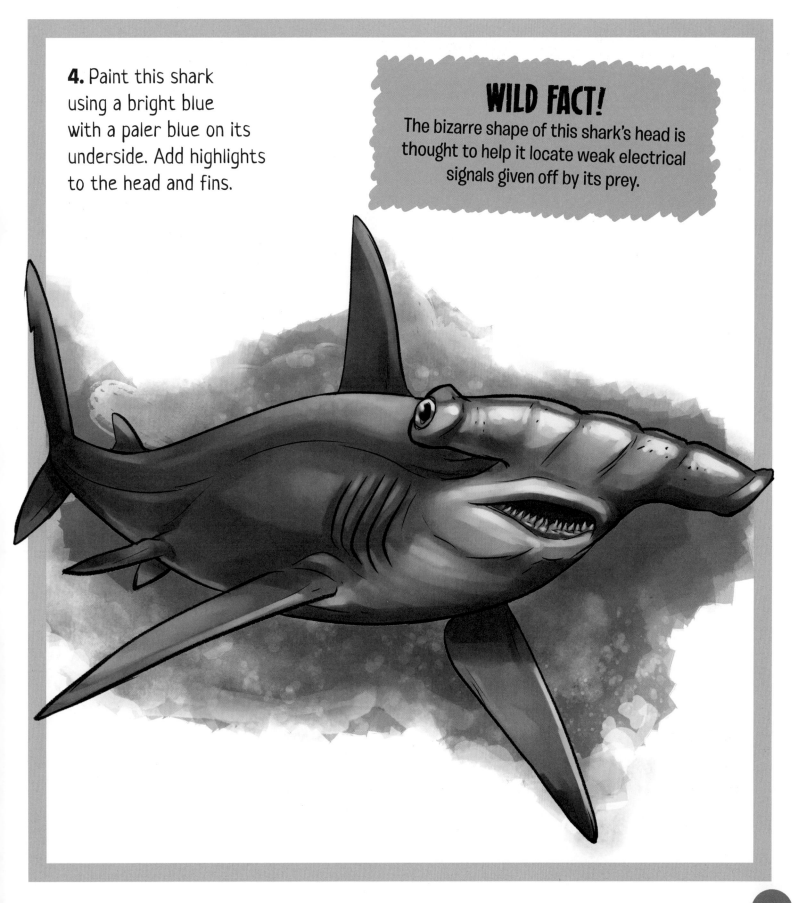

MANTA RAY

This gentle giant has a large mouth for scooping up tiny plankton.

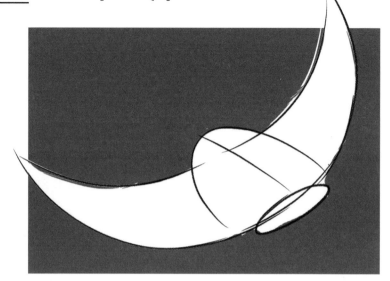

1. Sketch a crescent for the manta's pectoral (side) fins, with its wide, flat body in the middle and its open mouth.

2. Draw a tiny eye at the side of the head. Now draw the small fins below the mouth, which help it scoop up food, and a tiny dorsal fin on its back.

3. Draw the manta's thin tail, dividing lines on both pectoral fins, and the detail inside the mouth.

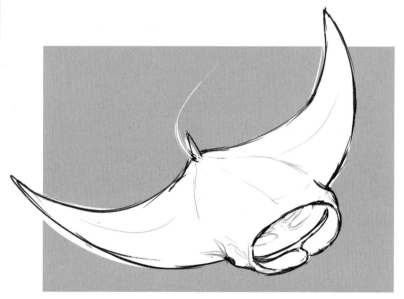

4. Mark the dark and light patches on the manta ray's body. The ray is dark on top and white on its belly.

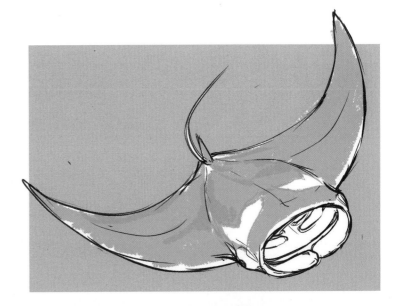

5. Use inky blue-black paint for the dark areas on the ray, leaving the fin tips, eyes, mouth, and symmetrical patches on either side of the head a pale blue.

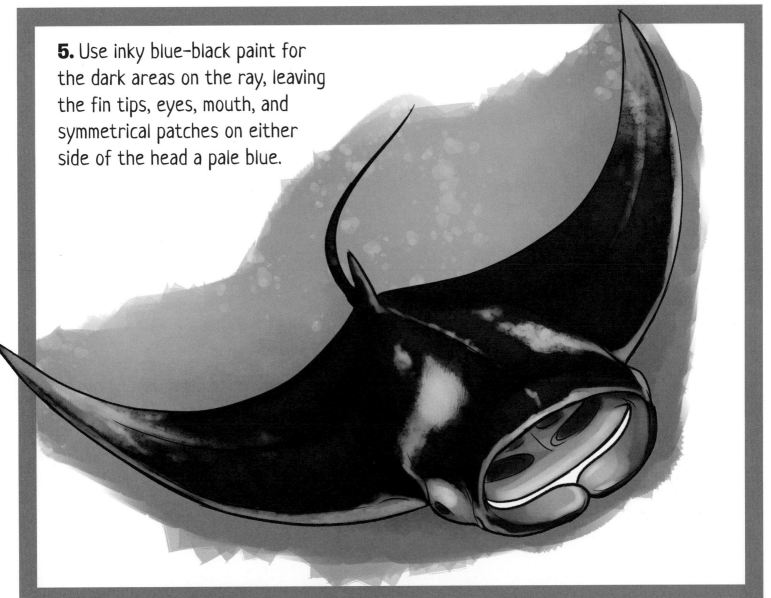

ORCA

The orca, or killer whale, is a large whale with a striking black-and-white pattern.

1. Draw a small oval for the head and a large oval for the body. Add a tall dorsal fin above, two paddle-shaped flippers below, and a tail leading to a wide fin.

2. Mark the open mouth, and add a tiny eye just above where the jaws meet. Add a curve in the tail.

3. Erase your working lines, and add some definition to the body, plus short, sharp teeth in the upper jaw.

4. Mark up the black areas on the orca's body, leaving a white belly and white spot behind the eye.

WILD FACT!

Like wolf packs, orcas work in teams to catch prey. They are often called "wolves of the sea."

HUMPBACK WHALE

This huge, bumpy humpback is swimming to the surface for air.

1. Draw a wide smile shape for the whale's body, then add in the fins and tail. Sketch in the head and curve of the body.

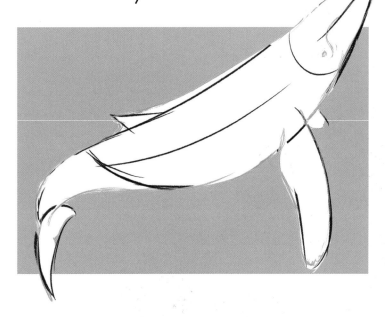

2. Position the small eye just behind and below the wide mouth. Join the body to the tail. Smooth out the line of the dorsal fin on the whale's back.

3. Give the side fin a bumpy edge. Draw small knobs, called tubercles, around the mouth. Shape the tail and front fin.

4. Paint your whale in a dark blue with a white and pale blue belly. Add some speckles on the side, fins, and head.

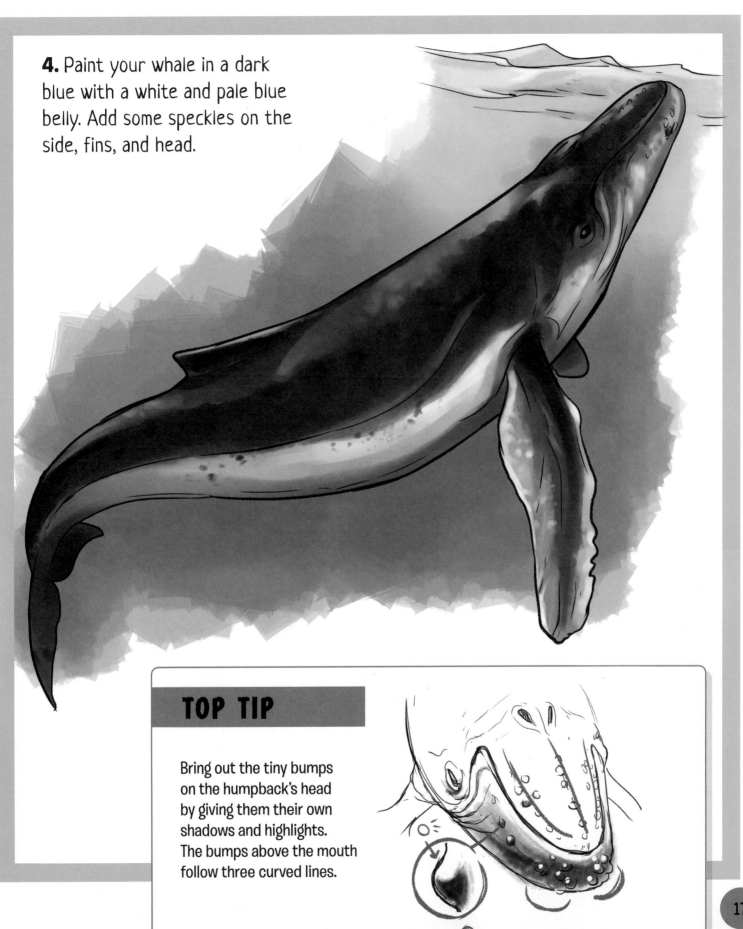

TOP TIP

Bring out the tiny bumps on the humpback's head by giving them their own shadows and highlights. The bumps above the mouth follow three curved lines.

NARWHAL

This unusual whale has a long, spike-shaped tusk on the front of its head.

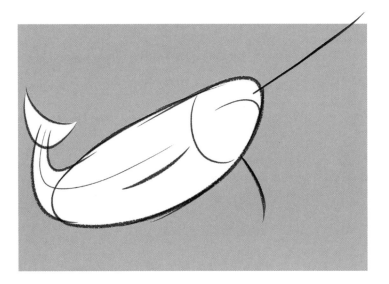

1. Draw an oval at an angle, with a curved tail on the left and a long spike on the right. Add lines for side fins and mark the head.

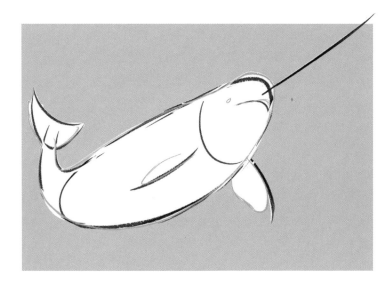

2. Shape the pair of rounded side fins, then position the small eye just behind the narwhal's wide mouth.

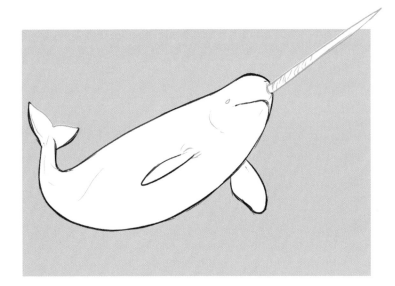

3. Shape the narwhal's tail, then add thickness to the tusk. Draw short lines up the length of the tusk for a spiral effect.

4. Lightly mark the areas of dark and light on the narwhal. It has dark side fins and a very spotty pattern over its body.

When creating the speckled pattern on the narwhal, go from large spots to smaller ones as you cross into the half with a different shade. Then, repeat in the opposite direction with the other shade.

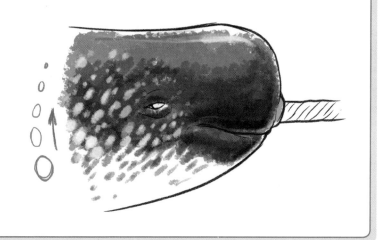

5. Use dark blue paint on the upper half of the narwhal and pale blue on the belly. Use these same shades to add spots on the opposite halves.

GREAT WHITE SHARK

One of the ocean's most powerful predators has a fearsome presence.

1. Draw a basic fish shape with a wide midsection. Mark where the back and side fins join the body, and also mark a tail and mouth.

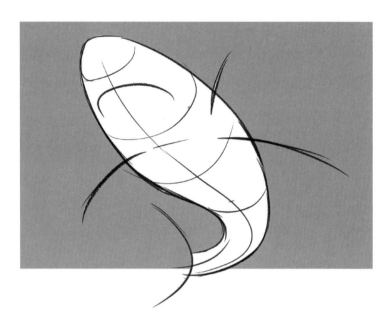

2. Shape the triangular fins and tail. Draw the outline of the open mouth, and place the eye.

3. Add the teeth, a pair of large nostrils, and the gill slits in front of the side fin. Note the four small fins near the tail.

4. Paint your shark with shades of blue, using a paler shade for the belly and dark pink for the gums.

TOP TIP

The great white shark has rows of jagged teeth that slowly move forward to replace those that break or fall out. You can draw these smaller extra teeth behind the front rows.

WHALE SHARK

The world's largest fish eats some of the sea's smallest creatures.

1. Start with a basic fish shape with a wide-open mouth. Draw lines to indicate the position of the fins and tail.

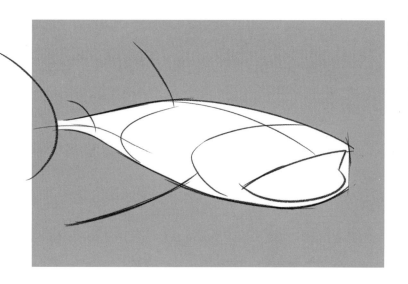

2. Shape the back and side fins. Sketch a small eye at the side of the whale shark's mouth.

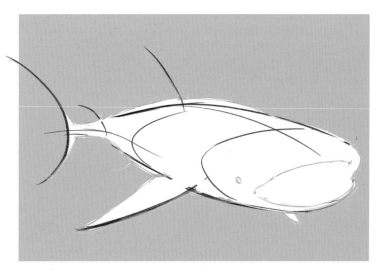

3. Complete the tail, then add three long lines along the body, gill slits behind the eye, and detail inside the mouth.

4. The whale shark has a spotted pattern, with white spots in bands from the tail and random spots on the head and fins.

5. Paint the upper side of the whale shark shades of brown with white spots. The belly is white and has the reflection of the blue sea.

WILD FACT!
The whale shark swims with its mouth open to take in millions of tiny plankton every day. It filters the water to pick out its food.

BASKING SHARK

This giant, harmless shark swims near the surface with a wide, gaping mouth.

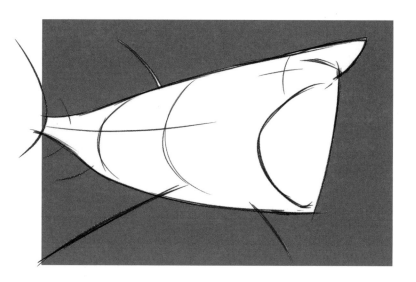

1. Start with a funnel-shaped body, with a wide-open mouth, pointed nose, and several long fins.

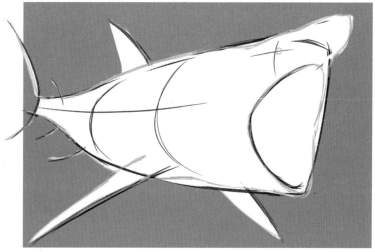

2. Shape the triangular fins and huge mouth. Position the eye above the mouth.

3. Draw curving gill slits halfway along the body, a nostril, and detail inside the mouth.

4. Paint your shark, adding a mottled pattern to the sides and back. There are bluish tones inside the large mouth.

TOP TIP

You may want to draw the same animal from different angles. It can be helpful to imagine rotating your picture to work out what you would see.

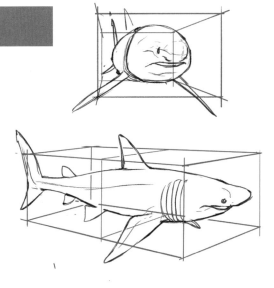

RELATIVE SIZES

If you want to draw several whales and sharks together in one picture, here's a handy chart that compares their sizes.

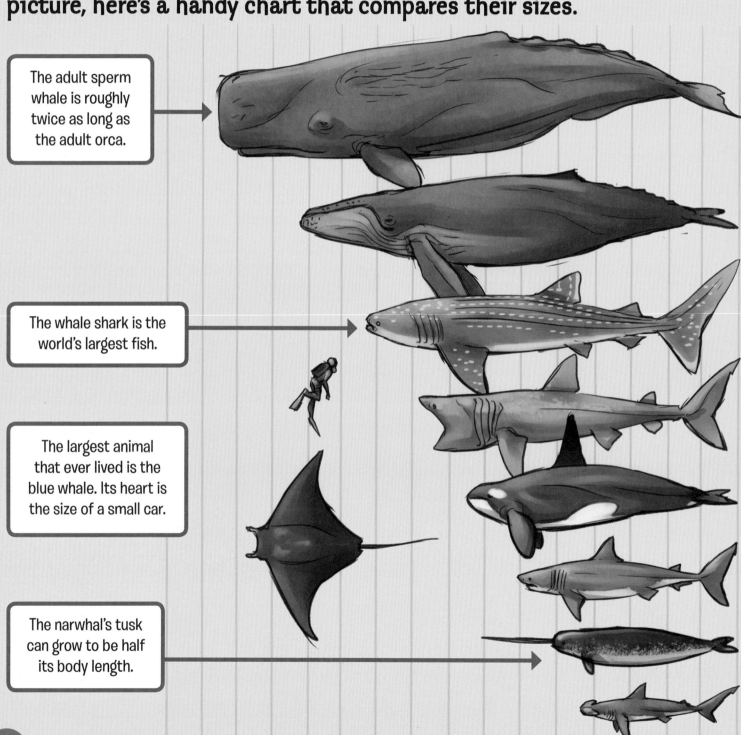

The adult sperm whale is roughly twice as long as the adult orca.

The whale shark is the world's largest fish.

The largest animal that ever lived is the blue whale. Its heart is the size of a small car.

The narwhal's tusk can grow to be half its body length.

OPEN WATERS

BLUE MARLIN

This fast-swimming fish has a tall fin and long, sharp bill.

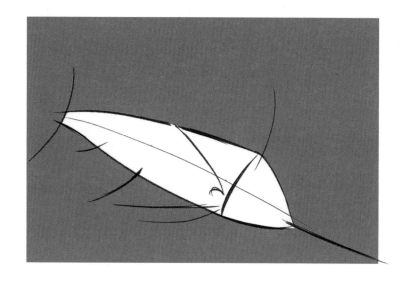

1. Start with a long fish body with a line along its middle. Add a thin spike from the nose and several lines indicating the fins and tail.

2. Shape the fins and tail, and draw the eye. Add the first gill slit behind the eye and a slightly open mouth.

3. Draw rays on the fins and tail and a line along the length of the body. Add detail to the head, including lines below the bottom jaw.

4. Paint the top half of the marlin a vibrant, inky blue. Use pale silver for the bottom half, with the hint of a sea-blue reflection.

WILD FACT!
The blue marlin is one of the fastest fish in the sea. It can reach speeds of up to 80 kph (50 mph).

GREEN TURTLE

This large sea turtle has a scratchy patterned shell and long front arms that are perfect for paddling.

1. Begin with a large leaf shape for the shell. Add two smaller leaf shapes for the rear flippers, two long, curving front flippers, and a flat-bottomed head.

2. The turtle's shell and each flipper should have a bumpy rear edge. Sketch the turtle's eye with wrinkly eyelids.

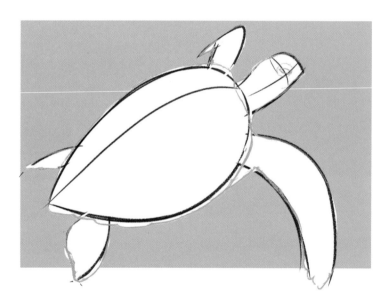

3. Carefully draw the shapes on the shell, starting with hexagons along the middle. Outline the scales over the flippers and head.

4. Paint the shell with patches of brown over turquoise. Each scale on the turtle's body is dark green with a thin, pale border.

TOP TIP

Look at photos of green turtles and study their shell patterns. Each section has a brown pattern pointing away from the middle of the shell like scratched paint.

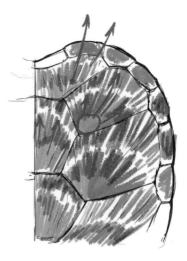

SUNFISH

This pale giant of the oceans looks like a huge fish head that is missing its body!

1. Start with a large C-shape, with a tall, curved line on the right and a small, rounded fin in the middle. Mark where the head will go.

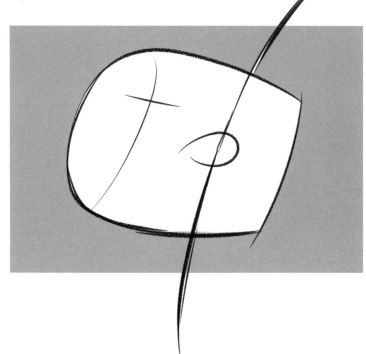

2. Outline the rear fins to look like knives. Place the eye toward the left side, and draw the open mouth.

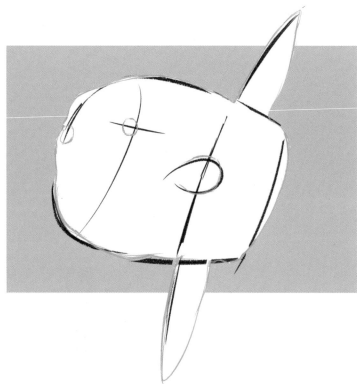

3. Give the tail and the fin on the right a frilly edge. Add a gill slit slightly above the fin and then draw wrinkle lines on the skin.

4. Use pale blue shades to paint your sunfish, adding darker shades along the bottom and around the wrinkles.

WILD FACT!
This huge flatfish got its name from its habit of swimming near the surface to sunbathe.

SQUID

The squid has a long body and large eyes, plus eight arms and two long tentacles covered in suckers.

1. Draw a long rocket shape with a rounded bottom. Add ten curvy lines for arms and tentacles that sprout from this rounded end. Mark in the fins at the other end.

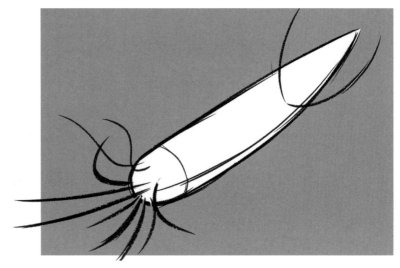

2. Add detail to the two curvy swimming fins at the back. Place the large, round eye, and add thickness to the arms.

3. Give the arms and the tips of the two tentacles lots of suckers. Draw a dark pupil in the eye.

4. Paint this squid using a lilac shade speckled with rusty spots. Add pale highlights along the edge of the body.

TOP TIP

When drawing fish eyes, draw a clear, dark pupil in the middle, then erase a small patch near the top. This is to show light reflecting from it.

BARRACUDA

This speedy, silvery fish has a mouth full of teeth that are like needles.

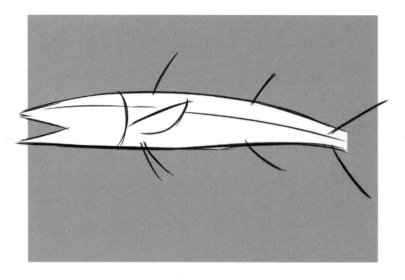

1. Draw a slim fish shape with a stripe along the body, open jaws, and lines showing the position of each fin.

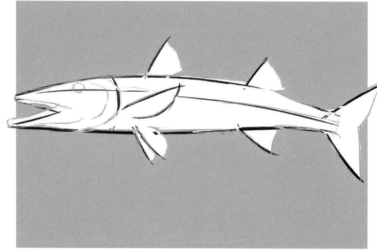

2. Outline all the small, pointed fins then add the eye and shape the tail. Add two curved lines for the gill slits.

3. Add lines inside each fin and the tail. Mark a pattern over the body for scales, then add spiky teeth and wrinkles.

4. The barracuda has a striped pattern along its upper half and darker edges on each fin.

The barracuda has very shiny skin.
To show this, use a lot of contrast in
your painting, with dashes of white
around the jaws, gills, and upper scales.

5. Paint your barracuda in shades of blue,
leaving a few white patches around the
mouth and as highlights on the scales.

FLYING FISH

This incredible fish has a pair of long side fins it can use as gliding wings.

1. Start with a basic fish shape with a V at one end. Add leaf shapes for the fins then mark the tail position.

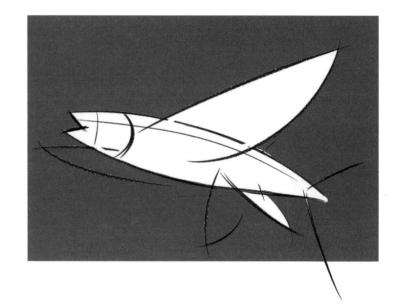

2. Draw the eye behind an open mouth. Fill out the shape of the fins and wide tail.

3. Add a pupil to the eye. Draw a fan of lines on every fin and the tail. Then, draw several wrinkle lines below the mouth.

4. Draw a simple pattern over the fish's body to mark its scales.

5. Paint the fish in silvery blues, with a shiny white stripe along its middle. The fins are a pale pink hue, with a series of darker shadow lines that follow each fin's fanned shape.

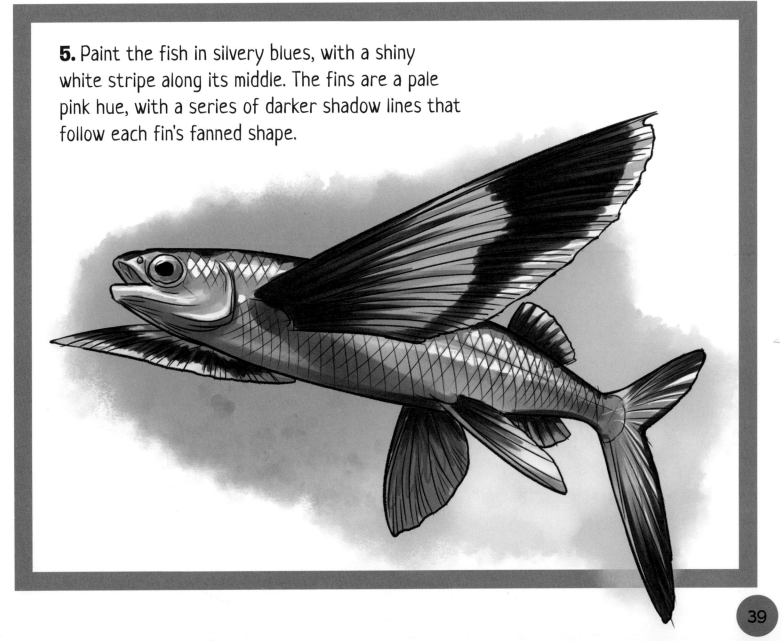

ANGLERFISH

To attract prey in the dark depths, this fish carries a glowing lure.

1. Draw a rough circle with a large section cut out for the jaws. Mark the tail, eye, lure, and fin positions.

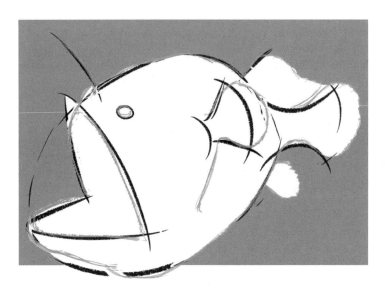

2. Shape the fins and give them a rougher edge. Add curves below the jaw.

3. Fill the jaws with teeth, and add a small bulb on the tip of the lure. Draw wrinkly lines over the body. Add fan lines to the fins and tail.

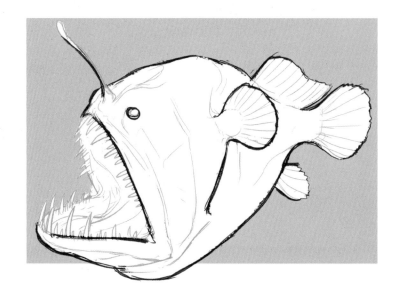

4. The anglerfish is a rusty brown with lots of tiny, paler spots. Paint the teeth and fins a pale charcoal.

TOP TIP

To show an anglerfish lighting up the dark, try using washes of white paint on black paper. The lure is the light source in this picture.

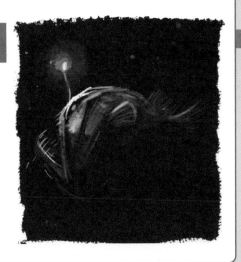

JELLYFISH

The soft-bodied jellyfish catches prey in its dangling and stinging tentacles.

1. Start with an umbrella shape for the jellyfish's bell, with several trailing lines for its tentacles. Add crease lines to the body.

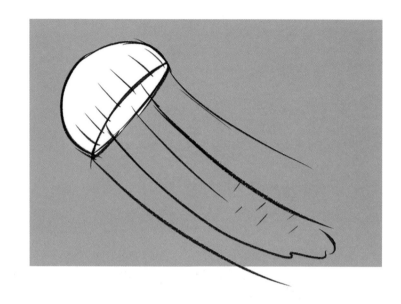

2. Thicken the tentacles, and give the bottom of the jellyfish's bell a bumpy edge.

3. Define the crease lines over the bell. Add a series of curly lines behind the tentacles for the jellyfish's arms, which resemble ribbons.

4. This jellyfish is a vibrant red orange. The arms are painted with a paler shade than the bell.

TOP TIP

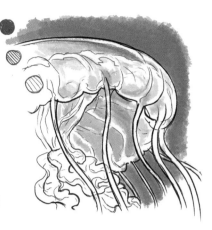

Many jellyfish are partly transparent—their mouth and stomach parts are visible through the bell. Use a softer pencil and paler shades of paint than with the rest of the jellyfish to reveal some detail.

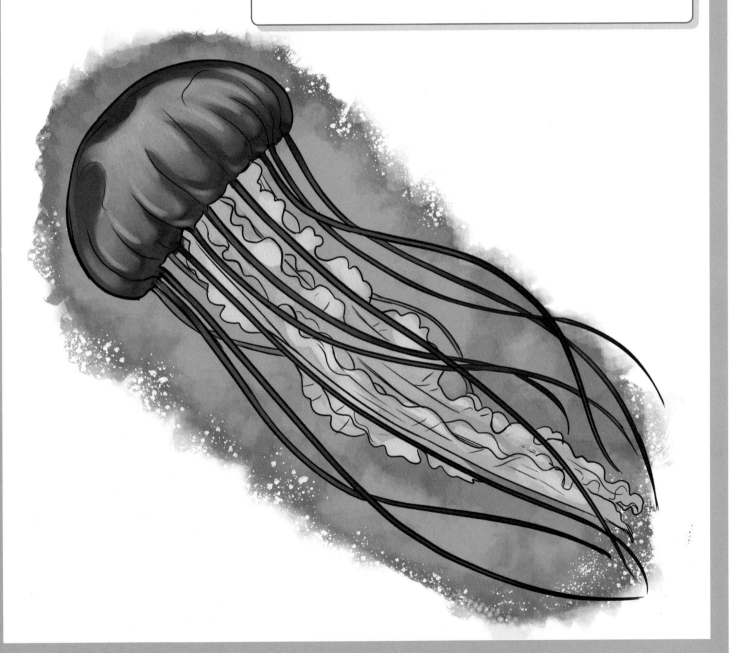

JOHN DORY

This fish has long, spiky fins, a wide mouth, and a distinctive spot on its side.

1. Begin by drawing an arrow shape with a tail attached. Draw long lines to mark where the fins will go. Also mark the positions of the eyes, mouth, and head.

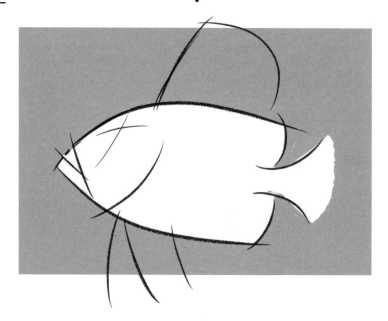

2. Add a fan of spines on the back (dorsal) fin. Sketch the eye and gill slits, and add a small fin behind this.

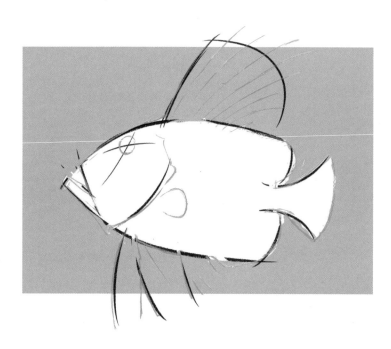

3. Give the fish lots of creases around the face. Add lines within the remaining fins. Mark a large spot on the side of the body.

4. Paint the John Dory in shades of olive green. Add darker fins and a dark spot on the side of the body.

NAUTILUS

This relative of the squid lives in a curved shell that it can hide inside.

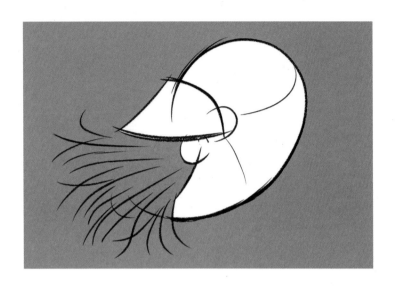

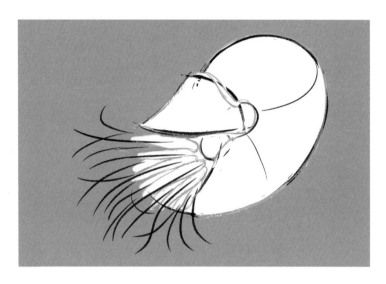

1. Start with a large comma shape for the shell, then add a hood on the left. Draw lots of wavy lines for tentacles.

2. Make the tentacles a little thicker near the shell, and shape the hood, adding a curve on the right.

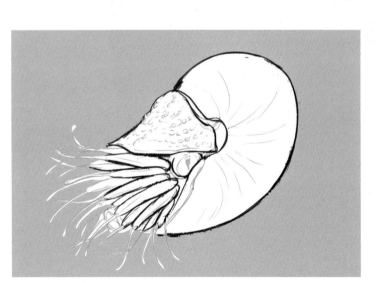

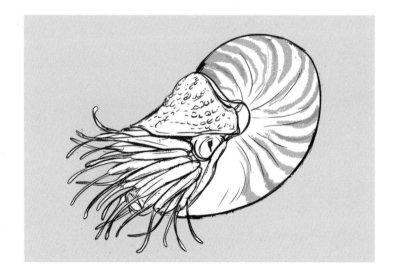

3. Sketch the eye and bumps on the hood. Round off the tentacles, and add a blowhole in their middle. Draw lines around the shell.

4. Thicken the lines around the nautilus shell to create a pattern of wavy stripes over it.

TOP TIP

The wavy stripes on a nautilus shell can vary. Some are thin and just cover only the top half of the shell. Others have thicker lines all over them.

5. Paint the nautilus a pale olive, then use a rusty red for the hood and stripes on the shell.

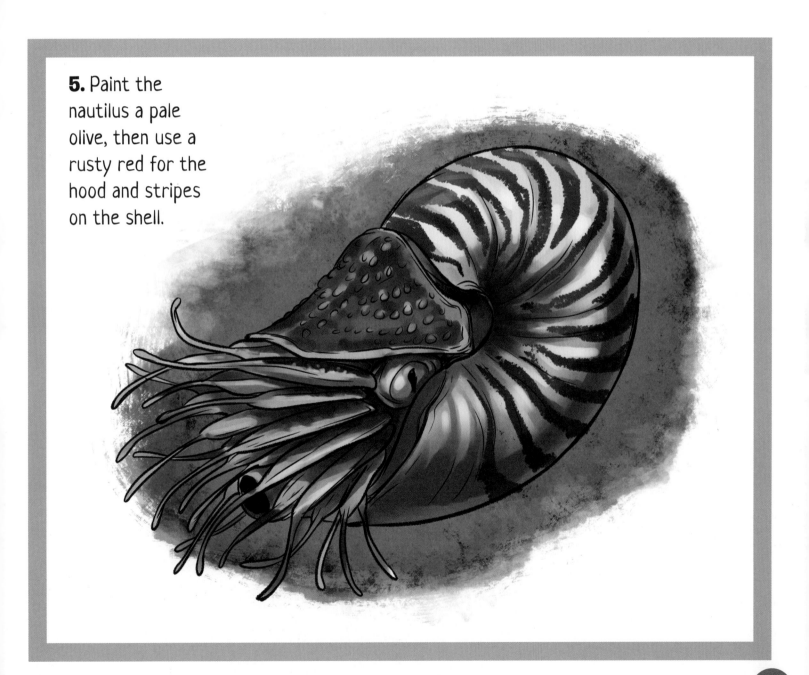

THE DEPTHS

Different fish live at different depths. Here is where you will find them.

Red light cannot reach below about 10 m (33 ft), so red sea creatures appear black below this depth.

The deeper you go, the less any light can reach. Some fish, such as the anglerfish, produce their own light to find food.

0-200 m (0-660 ft) SUNLIGHT ZONE

200-1,000 m (660-3,300 ft) TWILIGHT ZONE

1,000-4,000 m (3,300-13,100 ft) MIDNIGHT ZONE

CLOWN FISH

The bright clown fish lives beside an anemone, where it is protected by its stings.

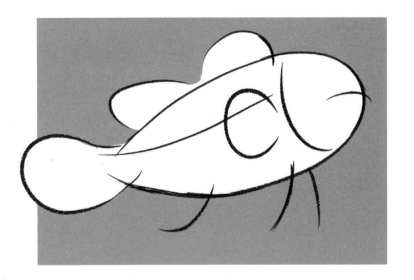

1. Begin with a basic fish shape, with a line from head to tail and rounded fins. Draw a mouth that curves down at the side.

2. Go over these lines, improving their shapes. Give the fins a slightly bumpy edge, and circle the eye above the mouth.

3. Dot the eye. Add an outline around the mouth, a fan of lines on the fins and tail, and wrinkly lines on the head.

4. Mark the dark stripes on the tail and back fins, plus the three wide, white stripes on the body.

5. The clown fish is bright orange with distinctive white stripes. Add some blue to the shadows on the white areas.

SEA HORSE

This delicate fish uses its curvy tail to cling to reeds and coral branches.

2. Divide the body into three sections along its length. Draw an eye and the tiny bumps on the head.

3. Draw lines across the body. Add a small bump where these lines cross the vertical lines and the edge of the body. Add detail to the fins and face.

1. Start by drawing a tall, curving body with a long snout, rounded belly, and a spiral tail. Add a fin on the back and another by the head.

WILD FACT!
Sea horses pair for life. But it's the male sea horse, not the female, that carries the eggs and gives birth to live young, called fry.

4. Paint this sea horse with yellow shades, adding some pale brown shadows inside each square section on the body.

TOP TIP

The sea horse's bony body appears as a raised grid pattern over its body, with bumps at every corner. Use shadows and highlights to bring out these raised areas.

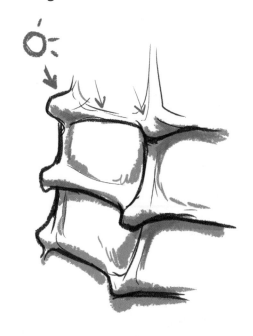

BANNERFISH

This stripy fish has a long, trailing dorsal fin. It likes to live in a large group.

1. Draw a circular body with a pointed mouth, one trailing back fin, several rounded fins, and a triangular tail. Mark the head position and add an eye.

2. Add detail around the mouth and eye. Draw fans of lines inside the fins and tail. Place groups of semicircular scales on the body.

3. Carefully mark the dark stripes on the bannerfish's body. The dark stripes cover some of the lower fins.

4. Use a bluish charcoal for the shadows and scales on the fish's body. Paint the stripes in a black wash. The side, back, and tail fins are yellow.

TOP TIP

The bony spines or rays on a fish's fins radiate from the point they join the body. This is a pelvic fin, usually found on the lower part of the body.

BLUE TANG

This bright fish has a flat body and markings that look like an artist's palette.

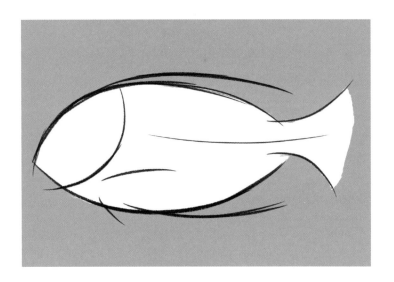

1. Start with an oval body joined to a triangular tail. Draw the position of the fins and the head.

2. Shape the fins, giving them a rounded edge. Circle the eye, and draw a small mouth on the lower half of the head.

3. Fill the tail and the fins with rows of short lines. Draw a pupil in the eye and the curved lines below the eye.

4. Mark the dark patterns over the blue tang's body, then mark the edges of its upper and lower fins.

5. Paint the blue tang with a blue body and darker blue pattern on the upper half. The tail has a yellow triangle in the middle.

PUFFER FISH

When in danger, the puffer fish takes in water to inflate into a spiny ball.

1. Start with a circle for the body, and add two small semicircles to indicate the position of the mouth and side fin.

2. Add the round eye and bottom lip. Draw the rounded fin to the right of the eye.

3. Add a pupil in the eye, lips around the mouth, and a fan of lines on the fin. Cover the puffer fish in spines that radiate out from the eye.

4. Give the fish a pale tan body with a light brown upper edge and a bluish reflection on the lower half. Add shadows below the lower spines.

TOP TIP

To position the puffer fish spines accurately, draw a series of circles around the body, and draw spines where the circles cross. The spines should point out from the imagined middle of the fish.

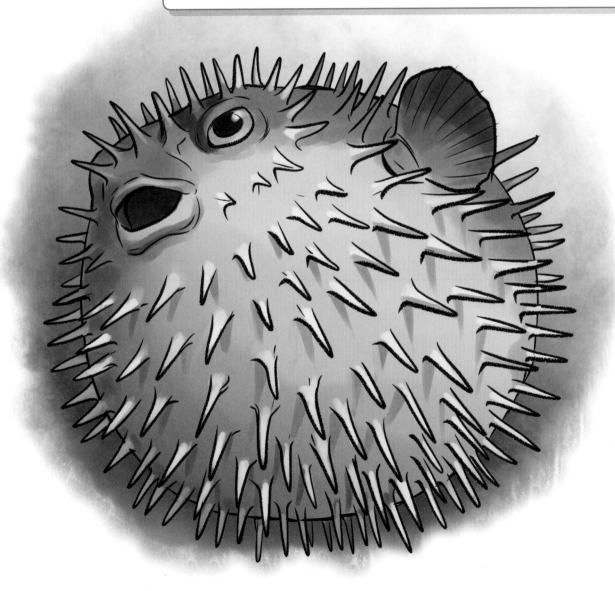

POTATO GROUPER

This fat-lipped fish has a blotchy pattern and can grow up to 2 m (6.6 ft) long.

1. Start with a basic fish shape, with a wide, downturned mouth and rounded fins.

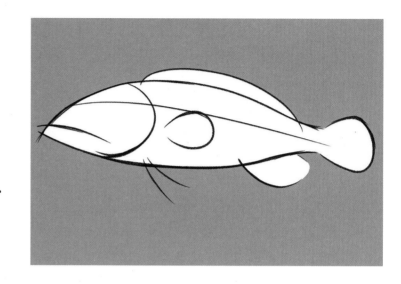

2. Add curves to the fins. Draw an eye near the front of the head and a slight gap in the mouth.

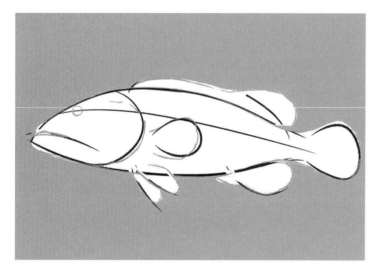

3. Give the fish wide lips and wrinkly lines below the mouth and to the right. Add fans of lines inside each fin and on the tail.

4. Mark the patterns on the grouper's body. It has dashed lines on the face and spots over the body and fins.

5. Paint the grouper's body with a light silver, adding a hint of turquoise to the shadows. The spots and lines on the face are shades of slate.

GIANT CLAM

Clams have two hard shells they can close to protect their delicate body.

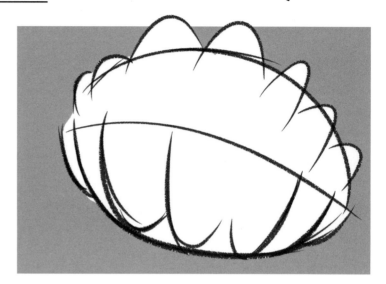

1. Draw an oval with a curved line across the middle. Add a row of bumps over the top and bottom halves.

2. Round off the bumps to form continuous curves. Draw two wavy lines over the dividing line.

3. Add a series of wavy lines over the outside of the shell halves and wrinkly lines on the inside.

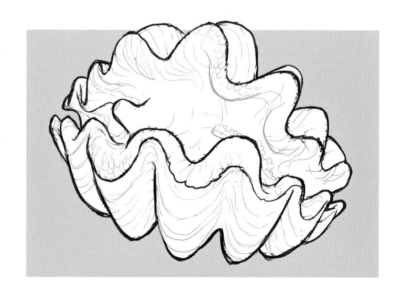

4. The clam shell is pale charcoal on the outside but full of bright blues and turquoise on the inside, with speckles on the rims.

WILD FACT!
The giant clam can weigh up to a whopping 225 kg (500 lb). It spends all of its adult life attached to a reef.

TRIGGERFISH

The titan triggerfish is protective of its nest and will chase away intruders.

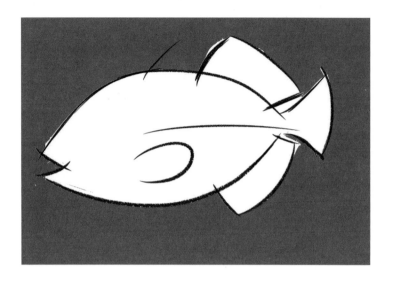

1. Start with a wide fish shape with a mouth and tail. Draw the fins at the top and bottom and mark in the other fins.

2. Refine the shape of the fins and tail. Add the eye, and shape the open mouth.

3. Add a pupil to the eye and lips around the mouth. Don't forget the teeth! Sketch lines to show the scales on its body.

4. Mark the patterns on the fish. This titan triggerfish has a dark mask, speckles on its scales, and dark fringes to its fins.

5. Paint the triggerfish with a mostly yellow body, adding dark brown patches on the scales and dark blue edges to the fins.

TOP TIP

When painting the diamond pattern of scales, go from dark on the left to a lighter shade on the right, leaving a little space between each diamond.

BUTTERFLY FISH

This bright yellow fish has a shape like the spade from a deck of cards.

1. Draw a heart shape on its side, with a triangular tail on the right. The fish has a rounded body and a pointed mouth.

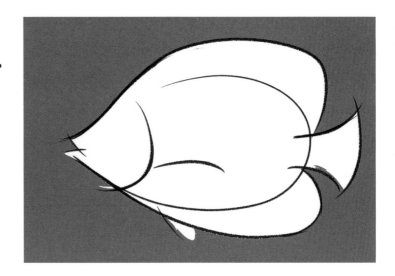

2. Give the fins a rough edge. Draw a large, round eye, curved gill slit, and a side fin.

3. Fill in the pupil of the eye, then add a fan of lines to the fins. Use diagonal lines in two directions to suggest the scales on its body.

4. The butterfly fish has a dark mask patch around its eye, several dark stripes across its body, and a dark fringe to its outer fins.

5. Paint the fish with a bright yellow body, charcoal mask, pale brown diagonal stripes, and thin, deep-blue lines on the fins.

MORAY EEL

This large marine eel hides in crevices waiting to ambush passing prey.

1. Start with two curving lines that form the numeral "8" on its side. Add an open mouth at one end and a tail at the other. Draw an upper fin along the body length.

2. Refine the shape of the long fin, and add a bulge below the head. Draw the open jaw and an eye.

3. Sketch folds where the eel bends, plus a few diagonal lines on the fins. Draw two bumpy nostrils and several sharp teeth in the open mouth.

4. Paint the moray eel with a lime green, adding greenish-blue shadows and a few blotches.

LIONFISH

This fish may look attractive, but the spines on its fancy fins are loaded with deadly venom!

1. Start with a basic fish shape, then add a series of curves around the body. This will indicate the positions of the fin rays.

2. Divide the fan shapes around the body into sections to mark individual spines. Draw the round eye.

3. Outline each spine. Draw a fan of lines on the tail fins. Add the growths above the eyes and over the mouth.

4. Lightly mark the zebra-type stripes and spots on the lionfish's body and spines. Use dotted lines on the tail fins.

5. Give the fish a very pale orange skin with rusty red stripes. Alternate wide and thin stripes on the body.

TOP TIP

You can be fairly free when painting the curvy stripes on the fish, filling gaps with thinner stripes. Note that the stripes continue over the eye.

COOL CORALS

Here are a selection of bright corals, sponges, and plants that you can try drawing. Add them to a scene featuring your best reef fish.

Sea fan

Finger coral

Anemone

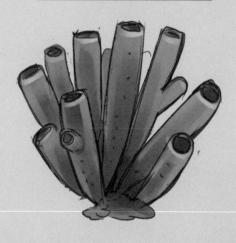

Tube sponge

Coral reef

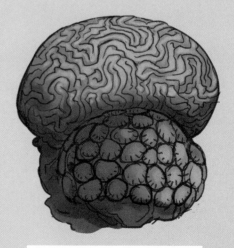

Brain coral

FIDDLER CRAB

Male fiddler crabs have one claw bigger than the other. They use the claw to battle other males.

1. Start with a pie shape joined to one small and one large claw. Mark the position of eight legs, two eyestalks, and a mouth.

2. Shape each leg, ending each with a point. Draw the eyestalks, and add a rounded eye at the tip.

3. Draw the segments on each claw and leg. Add the mouthparts, then add bumps next to the mouth and on the large claw.

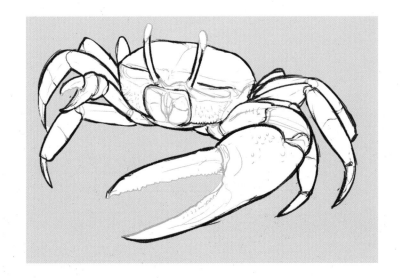

4. Paint the crab with a red-orange body and salmon-pink highlights. Use a dark brown for the eyes.

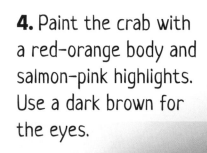

WILD FACT!

Fiddler crabs communicate by waving claws. The fiddler crab got its name because this waving motion made it look like it was playing a violin!

SEA LION

The sea lion is a mammal that can use its flippers both for swimming and for walking on all fours.

1. Begin with a curved, bean-shaped body. Shape the head and give the sea lion a snout. Add three visible, crescent-shaped flippers.

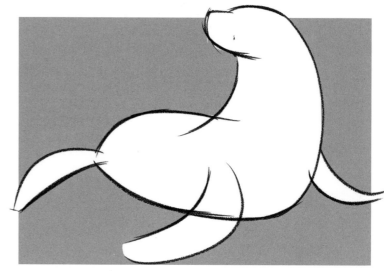

2. Round off the flippers. Give the sea lion an eye and an open mouth.

3. Divide the flippers into sections with "fingers." Add wrinkles around the neck and joints. Draw the sea lion's ear, teeth, and whiskers.

4. Paint the sea lion in dark shades, with some turquoise highlights that reflect the sea.

WILD FACT!

To tell a sea lion and a seal apart, look at their ears. Sea lions have visible ear flaps, while seals have just a tiny opening.

STARFISH

The five-legged starfish feeds through a mouth under the middle of its body.

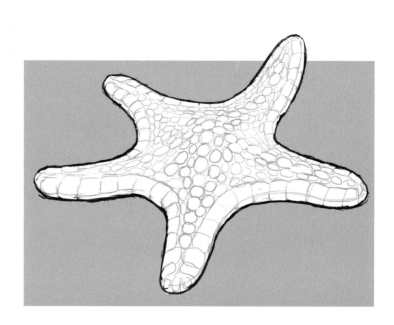

1. Draw five curving lines that rise where they meet in the middle, forming a star shape. Join them together with more lines.

2. Add a wide outline around the five legs, with a rounded tip at the end of each leg.

3. Draw brick-like segments around the edge of the starfish with lots of circles inside, across the whole body.

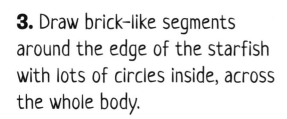

4. Give your starfish a pale orange body with bright orange edges and circular spots.

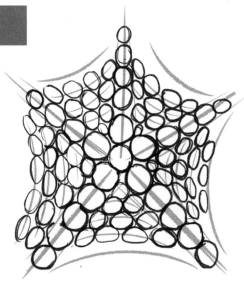

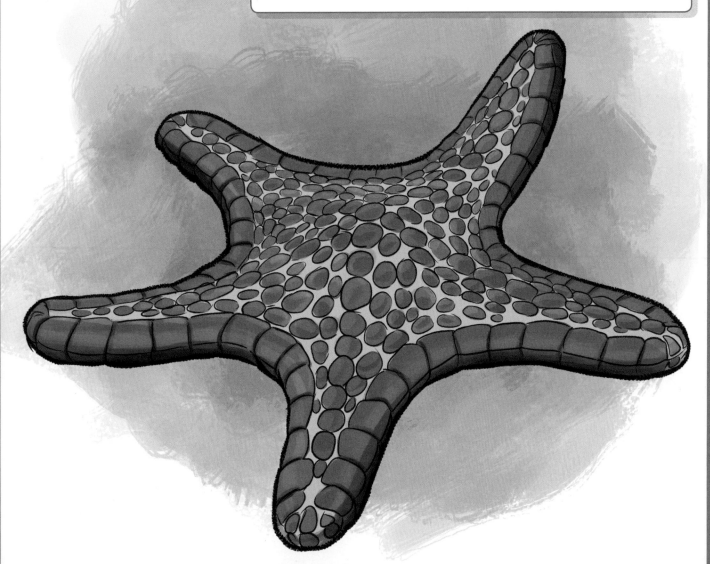

SEA OTTER

This sociable otter lives mostly in the ocean, kept warm by a dense layer of fur.

1. Sketch a large bean shape with a small head on the left, plus four curved legs and a wide tail on the right.

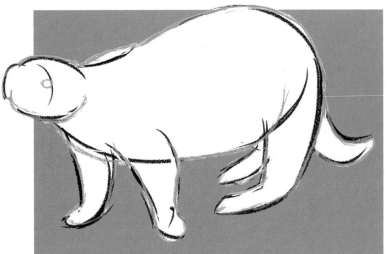

2. Refine the otter's body shape. Add an eye and a mouth.

3. Draw the nose, and add whiskers on either side. Add toes to the feet, then sketch tufts of fur over the body.

4. Paint the body with dark browns, using long, soft strokes in darker shades for furry shadows. Paint the head using a paler brown.

WILD FACT!
This otter rests by floating on the sea, often in a big group with other sea otters.

OCTOPUS

The octopus has eight arms with suckers underneath for gripping the seabed and reaching for food.

1. Draw a small oval for the head. Then, add four long, curling lines, plus another two lines to the left. They will become the arms at the back of the octopus.

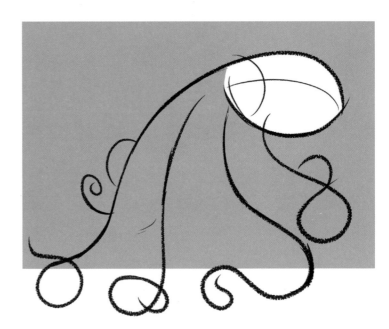

2. Widen these lines to make arms that start halfway down and end in point. Add two bulges for the eyes and two small tubes below the head.

3. Draw a U-shaped pupil in the eye. Sketch rows of suckers on the arms and texture on the body.

4. Paint the octopus bright red, with pink suckers and turquoise highlights on the arms.

TOP TIP

The suckers appear in two rows on the underside of each octopus arm. Draw them as short, stumpy tubes.

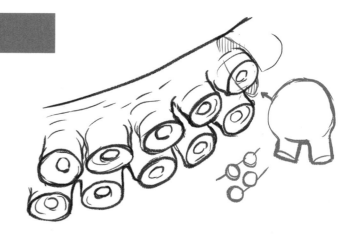

HERMIT CRAB

This small crab moves from one empty shell to another as it grows.

1. For a shell, draw a circle with smaller circles behind it. Add an oval for the shell opening. Then add two eyestalks and six legs.

2. Outline the joints where the legs meet the body, and draw four thin, curved antennae below the eyes.

3. Sketch the segments on the arms and claws, adding some very fine markings. Add detail to the eyes and shell.

4. Paint your crab a rusty red with a pale brown shade underneath. Decorate the cream shell with curved strokes in different rusty shades.

TOP TIP

Soft-bodied hermit crabs use shells left by other animals for protection. Here are some different shells you could draw for your hermit crab.

WALRUS

The heavyweight walrus lives on the Arctic ice and dives to the seabed to feed on clams.

1. Begin with a slug-shaped body with three visible flippers. Sketch the head, then add a mouth and two long curves for the tusks.

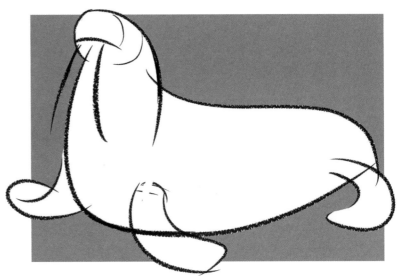

2. Shape the mouth and tusks. Add a small eye and toes on the tips of the flippers.

3. Draw lots of whiskery bristles above the mouth, then add wrinkles all over the body.

4. Paint the walrus pale brown, and bring out the wrinkles with a darker shade. Paint some mouth whiskers using white paint.

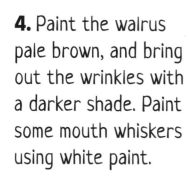

WILD FACT!
Male walrus tusks are used for display and for fighting other males. They can grow as long as 1 m (3.3 ft).

MARINE IGUANA

This iguana lives on the Galapagos Islands and feeds on underwater algae.

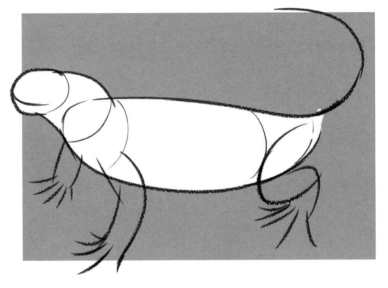

1. Draw a pea pod-shaped body. Add a rounded head, neck, long tail, and three visible legs with long toes.

2. Thicken the tail. Outline the clawed toes, and add a small eye.

3. Add a row of spines along the iguana's back and small, round bumps on the head. Sketch a few wrinkles and scales on the body.

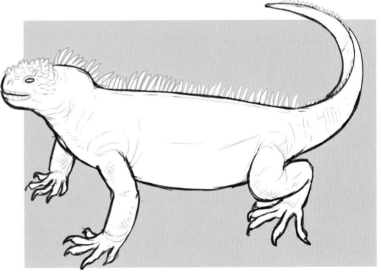

4. Paint the iguana a pale brown, then speckle the scaly body with dark browns, pale greens, and creams.

TOP TIP

Decorate the iguana's head with a series of scales around the eye and bumpier shapes on the forehead. Use crossed lines for scaly patterns elsewhere.

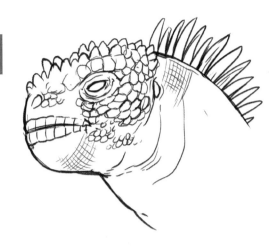

LOBSTER

The large-clawed lobster hides in crevices on the seafloor.

1. Draw a three-part body with two large claws, four thin pairs of legs, and long antennae.

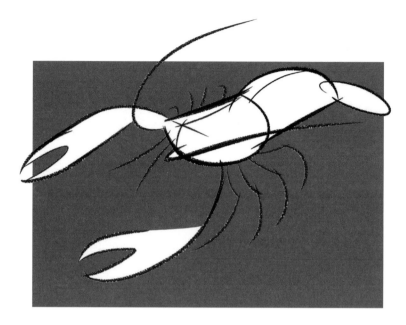

2. Shape the front claws, legs, and antennae. Add two small eyes and feeding parts on the head.

3. Outline the segments on the legs, claws, and tail. Give the claws a serrated edge.

4. Paint the lobster a deep red, with a pale orange underbelly and pale brown legs. Speckle the lobster's shell with dark red spots.

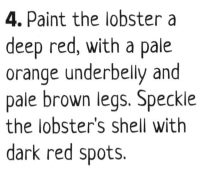

WILD FACT!
Lobsters, like spiders and snails, have blue blood!

91

MANATEE

The manatee is sometimes called a sea cow. It grazes on plants that grow on the seabed.

1. Start by drawing a semicircular body with a rounded head, triangular nose, two flippers, and a wide tail.

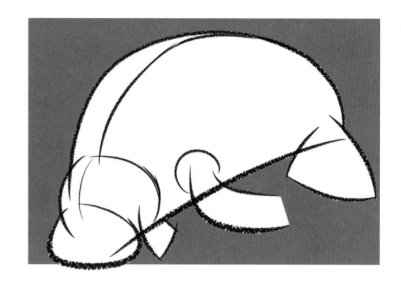

2. Refine the body and flipper shapes. Draw a small eye and a pair of nostrils.

3. Split the upper lip in two, and add whiskers on each side. Sketch wrinkles over the body and joints. Draw some greens in the mouth.

4. Paint the manatee a dark shade. Give the animal a speckly finish with shadows, plus cream and green highlights over the upper body.

TOP TIP

The manatee's bulky body shows many folds. These follow the curve of its body, its joints, under its chin, and outward from the eyes.

SEAL PUP

Seal pups are born with thick white fur, which keeps them warm and helps them hide on ice.

1. Draw a curving body and head. Add a small circular nose, plus two front and two rear flippers.

2. Add a pair of large, round eyes, nostril slits, and a curved mouth. Shape the body and flippers.

3. Add toes to the flippers and whiskers on the top lip. Use rows of short lines to create furry folds on the body.

4. Paint the seal pup with a creamy white. Use darker paint to show the texture of the fur. Don't forget to add dots of white in each of the pup's eyes.

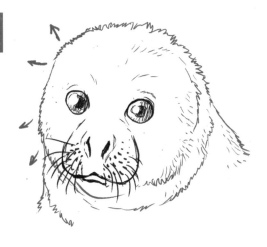

UNDERWATER WORLD

Now that you've made a start drawing the sensational sea creatures in this book, you can keep going.

You don't have to be a deep-sea diver to draw sea creatures from life. Take your sketchbook to a zoo or an aquarium, where you'll find plenty of underwater wonders to doodle!